HOW DO I HATE THEE?

How Do I Hate Thee?

A Sampler of Poetic Rage Against Cancer

by Elizabeth Kincaid-Ehlers

Elizabeth Kincaid Ehlers

Antrim House

Simsbury, Connecticut

Library of Congress Control Number: 2011936182

ISBN: 978-1-936482-08-5

Printed & bound by United Graphics, Inc.

First Edition, 2011

Cover photograph by the author

Photograph of author by Jordan Rueckert

Book Design by Rennie McQuilkin

The poem "Rage, Idle Rage" was first published in *Caduceus*

Antrim House
860.217.0023
AntrimHouse@comcast.net
www.AntrimHouseBooks.com
21 Goodrich Road, Simsbury, CT 06070

ALSO BY ELIZABETH KINCAID-EHLERS

Seasoning: Poems 2005-2009 (Antrim House, 2009)

Leaping and Looming: Collected Poems 1979-2004 (Merganser Press, 2005)

River's Edge: A Sampler of Poetry (Merganser Press, 1985) — poems by Poets of the River's Edge: Charles Darling, David Holdt, Susan Gimignani Lukas, and Elizabeth Kincaid-Ehlers.

Waterscapes: A Sampler of Poetry (Merganser Press, 1986) — more poems by Poets of the River's Edge.

The author's literary and psychological essays have appeared in numerous university and medical journals and books. They include the following:

"Bad Maps for an Unknown Region: Menopause from a Literary Perspective," *Changing Perspectives on Menopause,* ed. A. Voda, M. Dinnerstein and S. O'Donnell, University of Texas Press, Austin, Texas, 1982, pp. 24-38.

"'Oh dear me! Why weren't we all boys, then there wouldn't be any bother': Menarche and Popular American Fiction," *Menarche: The Transition from Girl to Woman,* ed. Sharon Golub, Lexington Books, D.C. Heath and Co., Lexington, Massachusetts, 1983, pp. 205-222.

ACKNOWLEDGMENTS

I want to thank:

Dr. Sally Ardolino, for caring for me over the years and for spotting the invader when she did.

Dr. Mark Dailey, for dealing with lymphoma and me at the same time — not an easy task.

Donna Rioux—who has repeatedly outwitted my "dainty veins" in order to get my infusions going—for her extraordinary patience and amazing aim.

All the people at the Helen and Harry Gray Cancer Centers in Hartford and Avon; they are a marvelous group of caring folks.

My sons and their wives: Quentin and Mandie, Jordan and Kate, and Morgan and Rorie. They know all that they do and what they have to put up with. I hope they really do know how grateful I am for everything. And Theron and Kay, for calling and caring, from farther away.

Special friends who have gone out of their way to help: Liz, for taking me to my first infusion and helping me learn the ropes; Louise, for long and patient talks and even some visits; Sybille, for hanging in there; Marilyn and Sherri for helping to keep the poetry going; and Sally, who helped keep my expressions of anger in check.

Those friends and colleagues and clients and former clients who have, truly, held me in their hearts and understood. You know who you are.

and, lastly though never leastly:

David and Drew, who have stayed the course and finally convinced me that they not only liked what I have done with the poems, but thought other readers and poets and patients would, as well. Can you believe?

To Abbie, Ashley, Sadie, Will, Sammy, Kyle and Jackson —

may they strive and thrive

TABLE OF CONTENTS

PREFACE

When I was first diagnosed with 3rd stage non-Hodgkins Lymphoma, I went into a mild form of shock—not, I am told, an unusual reaction. Then, being me, I said, "So be it. Let's get real here. How do I fight it?"

Undergoing chemotherapy is not fun. I believe that anyone who experiences this particular trip will agree. All the same, I am grateful that such treatment exists. As I am grateful for all the physical and moral support I have received. Honestly, I believe that I am one of the lucky ones.

So I myself was surprised at my response to certain comments I received from folks who appeared to wish me well. More than one came up to me, asked how I was and, without really listening to my response, made a dismissive gesture and said, ever so brightly, "Oh, I'm sure you'll be just fine." I became aware of deep anger arising in me whenever something like this happened. And my response gave rise to an entirely new awareness, both of my own reality and of the healing power of anger.

Healthy anger is not negative. It helps us focus energy that can be used to resist, to fight, to overcome. Repressed anger creates depression. Or a dissociation that leads to unreality. Neither condition will aid in healing.

Some people deal with simple reality better than others. Some are afraid to feel their own fear or their own anger or to deal with uncertainty. They seem to hold all threats off by an automatic "Oh, I am sure you'll be fine." Such responses are not helpful. In my case, they opened up my anger.

If you say you hope I will recover, or get better, or that my treatments will be as comfortable as possible, I will appreciate your caring and concern. If you say you pray for me, or carry me in your heart, or hold me in the light, I will be grateful. Touched. Comforted.

When you drive me to treatments, and wait, and drive me

back home again, you help remind me why life is worth living. When you drop off soups and bread and salads and home-baked almost anything, my heart fills, and peace and goodness spread. Just do not tell me that everything will be fine.

I explained to as many people as I could—that is, to those who were receptive—how the reflexive dismissal touched my anger and was not helpful. Many listened and learned. Some never will.

Still, something very useful to me has come from all these encounters. I have learned about my own anger and I have found ways to deal with it. Enlisting some of my favorite poets and favorite poems, I have come upon a way to rage creatively and safely. I have used the energy unleashed by my anger to fight cancer. I have become a hardy contender.

Elizabeth Kincaid-Ehlers
West Hartford, Connecticut
August 1, 2011

GRATITUDES

The author is grateful to those authors whose works she has transformed. She hopes they might be consoled when they understand that, as she has been humming to herself during the months, now years, of working on this project, she "only hurts the ones she loves."

All honor then to:

W. H. Auden
William Blake
Elizabeth Barrett Browning
Robert Burns
Geoffrey Chaucer
e.e.cummings
Emily Dickinson
John Donne
Robert Frost
Robert Herrick
Gerard Manley Hopkins
John Keats
Ruggiero Leoncavallo
Richard Lovelace
Archibald MacLeish
John Masefield
Dorothy Parker
Edward Arlington Robinson
Theodore Roethke
William Shakespeare
Percy Bysshe Shelley
Wallace Stevens
Alfred, Lord Tennyson
Dylan Thomas
Anna Bartlett Warner / Susan Warner
William Carlos Williams
William Wordsworth
James Wright
Sir Thomas Wyatt
William Butler Yeats
and anonymous

FOREWORD

The Waiting

All these years
herons have owned our bay.
Descendents or conquerors,
no way to know for certain.
Each one squawks with rage
when I go down to swim.
"Mine! Mine! Mine!"
it screams as it slowly flops
off the rock, goes low across
the water and up, flap,

flap to a branching oak
where it perches, watching.
Oh, it will be back.
Back to stand again
upon the rock, quiet,
all the time in the world
to get that minnow, frog,
or lively, shining fish.
Like cancer, all it has
to do is patiently wait.

HOW DO I HATE THEE?

Big Lymphoma

Whenever Big Lymphoma came to town
We missed his entrance, never noticed him.
Had we glimpsed him we'd have shot him down.
Instead we catered to his every whim.

Oh, he was so hidden, so discreet.
No one even heard him when he talked.
His true glory is to steal and cheat.
Damn, I wish he'd glittered when he walked.

And he is strong — yes, stronger than a king —
Kong, I mean, not one who's schooled in grace.
Truth is, we missed him, never noticing
The tip-offs, clues to help us make a case.

So we went on, and on, and on, and on.
And lost all taste for meat and even bread.
Let's hope that Big Lymphoma, come the dawn,
Comes out and puts a bullet through his head.

Cancer Is A'coming In

Cancer is a'coming in,
 Loud sing cuckoo!
Grows in cells, plunks me in hells
 And crams my body, too.
Shout "you hoo."

Mothers sing over babes,
 Chase after sons and Dad.
Friends jump... Infusions pump,
 Cancer struts: "I'm bad."
"You hoo." "You hoo!"

And stop you never, too.

Shout "you hoo," now shout "you hoo."
Shout "you hoo," shout "you hoo!" now.

On First Being Diagnosed Stage Three

Sorely had I been tested by disease,
Bad luck and accidents and stunts insane;
Down different roads I'd dragged my damaged knees,
Trying out crutches and a hand-carved cane.
For weeks I lay in bed seeking ease,
Waiting to see if polio's power would wane.
Yet had I never faltered, nor begged "please,"
Till I heard "Lymphoma" clear and plain.
Then felt I like some infant, lone, forlorn,
Shot from the womb into a world of fear.
Not an explorer greeting each new morn
Or zesty traveler testing fine new gear:
Rather a miscreant, caught, and none to mourn,
Strapped, entombed, on funeral tower drear.

Rondel of Merciless Hurt

Your great big cells might win eventually;
Their creeping stuns me who was once serene;
All through my gut the wounds are slow and mean.

Only your death would heal the injury
To my dumb innards. Oh, so long unseen —
Your great big cells might win eventually;
Their creeping stuns me who was once serene.

No fear, I honor your intensity,
And know you sometimes kill both quick and clean
With all the ammo in your magazine.
Your great big cells might win eventually;
Their creeping stuns me who was once serene;
All through my gut the wounds are slow and mean.

Bigger Lymphoma

I thought he'd traveled from a far-off land
To let me know how merciless his power,
For when he finally popped and showed his hand
My life was leaking out, hour by hour.
No doubt that moment who is in command,
Who holds the reins, the whip, the gouging spurs;
Who breaks trail ever onward far and sings —
And whom no troop or fortress yet deters.
He'd like to have a pedestal carved like this:
"My name is Big Lymphoma, King of Kings:
Look on my works, ye Mighty, my ass kiss."
No one would remain, just dangling rope.
And yet, there stirs in *this* colossal wreck,
a sprout of laughter and a sprig of hope.

Spotted Rashy

All praise to Cancer for our spotty rash —
For skins of multi-dots like cartoon cats;
Or bump moles speckled upon burping toads;
Dappled, indeed, and hoarded in a stash;
Laid out in mazes — wrinkles, folds, flats;
      All sizes, babes, geezers, armloads;
Everywhere original, gross, eye-popping;
You could not imagine such tats, gnats;
Quick strokes and scattered dashes, secret codes
He makes up whose power is past stopping.
      Honor Him.

J.D., You Go and Catch a Star

J.D., you go and catch a star,
or make some tea from mandrake root.
I'm stuck chasing falling hair
and, frankly, do not give a hoot.
As for mermaids, you should see
the rash that's blistering all of me.
Envy's not the cause of stinging.
Go look
for what took
my mind and shredded my new book.

You want strange sights? Try purple bruises
where Rituxan drip infuses.
Lie back for interminable hours
while white hairs shed in crunchy showers.
Then help me haul my pole to pee,
and say how good I look to thee.
You'll swear
you care
and I'll stay this side of despair.

If you have hope, spare me some —
just don't say you know I'll be fine.
I'm not stupid — maybe numb —
I'll never fall for the smiley face line.
Lymphoma's a persistent foe,
knows just where it wants to go,
and fights
for its rights
all my days and all my nights.

The White, White Dandelion

Your love may be like a red, red rose
blooming ripe in June;
I have become a dandelion
drooping 'neath the moon.

No one could call me fair, alas,
unless a giant, sowing,
would pluck me up and hold me tight
and pass some time by blowing.

You did it when you were a lad —
bairns still do it, vying:
they blow and blow and laugh like mad
'til all the fluff is flying.

Well, fare-thee-well, I'm not yet gone.
The rock stays hard in the sun.
I hope to sing again, come dawn,
while the sands of life still run.

No Comment

Oh, I can smile and beam at all
who exclaim how wonderful I look
while assuring me life will be a ball
and Mr. Lymphoma is not a crook.

Snapshot

Elizabeth's
defunct

      who used to
      write a sunshinepolished
              opening

and flaunt onetwothreefourfive rhymewordsjustlikethat
                                    Jesus
she was a blazing broad

           and what i want to know is

how do you like your greeneyed girl

Mister C

The Tyrant of Lymphoma

Call up the strutter of hairpiece and suits,
The thickened one and watch him poke
In hidden rooms his secret cells.
Let the kids dress up in play clothes
Pretending wild things or astro guides,
Drawing curlicues with crayons.
Let seem be the last newcomer.
The only ruler is the tyrant of Lymphoma.

Sneak from that old cherry dresser,
That one with the knobs that keep working loose,
The hankies that once were her Mom's and Dad's,
And drape them over her droopy face.
If her crooked feet stick out, then shout
To show you know the miles she walked.
Let lights go out. Yup. A Bummer.
The only ruler is the tyrant of Lymphoma.

Sneak, Sneak, Sneak

Sneak, sneak, sneak,
  Into my nodes, Big C!
And I would that my mind could fathom
  The rage that arises in me.

O well for the neighbor's children
  That run and jump and ride.
O well for the morning walkers
  who swing and strut and stride.

And the ship of life goes on
  To that harbor beyond the hill.
O for a chance to grab the wheel
  And sail 'til I've had my fill.

Sneak, sneak, sneak,
  Out of my nodes, Big C!
Though the innocence of the life that was
  Will never come back to me.

Like Her, I Said To Hell with Death

Like her, I said to hell with Death —
He's coming after me —
He rides behind, not by my side,
Not wanting all to see.

We're creeping on — He doesn't care —
I'm loath to put away
My work, my loves, my pleasures, too,
For his Intensity.

We travel to the specialists —
They claim they do not see Him.
I talk to others in the room,
Watch as their lights go dim.

I track the sun, the moon, the stars —
Feel Winter's gathering chill —
I am but skin and cramping bones
And ever-increasing ill.

We slow outside a hospital —
It claims to salvage life —
That hope is scarcely viable
And I am punched toward strife.

Since then, seems centuries, and yet
Three months have passed, no more,
Since first I knew this bastard's leer
Already through my door.

I Thought I'd Master'd the Trodden Ways

I thought I'd master'd the trodden ways
   Over the mountain and back,
Every two months on the first of Fridays,
   I got the knack.

Then shingles took advantage of me
   All across one eye —
Slammed me about in misery —
   Actually made me cry.

Into the hospital I had to go,
   Then out to wait and see.
Lymphoma's probably growing, and, oh,
   The difference to me!

Cancer, Get Over It

Cancer, get over it. Although you think you're swell,
You're nothing special, just an oddity
To those you think will die by your decree,
A bloody nuisance to us in whose nodes you dwell.
Just because you wield a mighty cell
You fancy Death is bowing low to Thee.
Poor Cancer — enjoy your serendipity —
Or go ahead, strut and boast and yell.
You're only one of Death's accoutrements.
Next to nuclear war you're just a pest,
A paltry piffle, an infinitesimal jest
To those who stay the course as bon vivants.
Everyone ends in that last short sleep.
Death will beat you C, you pitiful creep.

The River Island of Set Me Free

I'll try to get up and go now, go to the Isle of Stave.
To my cabin already built there, of cedar and oak and pine.
Tall hickories grow there, homes for black squirrels I crave.
And I'll stay alone, as I used to, in the haven that was mine.
I'd like to have some peace there, without the fear and pain:
Fear turns nights to mourning for loss of what I've been
And pain turns noon to midnight, all hopes for light in vain,
Makes memories a trash pile, a smile a raucous grin.
I'll try to get up and go now, if only in fitful dream,
For I hear the River slapping the dock and rocks by the shore.
A lone loon calling, an osprey's sudden scream,
Will be enough to heal me, at least in my heart's deep core.

Cancer Loves Me, This I Know

Cancer loves me! This I know
For the CAT Scan tells me so.
My gut cells to Him belong.
I am weak and He is strong.

> Yes, Cancer loves me!
> Yes, Cancer loves me!
> Yes, Cancer loves me!
> My CAT Scan tells me so.

Cancer loves me! This I know
As he loved so long ago.
Taking people on his knee
Saying "I'll take them with me."

> Chorus

Cancer loves me when I'm good
Taking treatment as I should.
Cancer loves me when I'm bad
'Cause He knows I can be had.

> Chorus

Cancer loves me! He won't die
And he'll never answer "Why?"
He will take his pick and choose
Who will win and who will lose

> Chorus

The Sneak That from the Old Root Sucks the Flower

The sneak that from the old root sucks the flower
Sucks my old age; that undercuts the hills
Is my death-sower.
And I will loudly shout, in harshest shrills,
"My last years are seared by this fever."

The sneak that sucks the rivulets from rocks
Sucks my tired blood; that crumples all my dreams
Corrupts the facts.
And I will scream no matter who disdains
To know about my horror as the sneaker sucks.

The fist that smashes healers from the marsh
Whips up quicksand: that stops the winds of hope
Grinds mine to ash.
And I am loud and louder to proclaim
How of my cells is made the killer rope.

The nails of nature rip what nature makes;
Love strokes and pats, perhaps can even knead
The pain away.
Yet I will bellow to the roaring wind
How cancer tricks the body to betray.

I'll not be dumb. I'll warn whoe'er will heed
How in our plots are sewn those sneaky seeds.

This Is Not To Say

I have beaten
the cells
that were in
my body

and which
were most definitely
intending
to kill me.

Bear with me.
They are tenacious,
so sneaky
and so strong.

This Time of Life

This time of life thou mayst in me behold
When wispy hairs, or none, or few, do hang
Upon this skull, which puckers in the cold,
Bare bones to cause old friends to hide the pang.
In me thou seest the fading of a life
That once was driving hard from dawn to dusk.
Now bit by bit it goes beneath the knife
Diminishing 'til all that's left is husk.
In me thou seest the fading of a light
That in the brightening of my youth did shine,
And in its birthing thought there'd be no night,
No death, no matter how stars might align.
This I perceive and this I try to say:
Please let us love before I go away.

Under Night's Cover

When in the night Lymphoma grows
I lie and think nobody knows
How lushly cancer sows and mows.

Then, when I rise, alive, to see
Just how Lymphoma's altered me,
I demand the invader set me free.

River Sickness

I'll not get up to the River again, to the open water and sky,
With islands out there far and farther to see before I die.
My boat stays tied to the dock now, covered in canvas and grime.
I thought I would steer her forever, never run out of time.
I cannot go up to the River again, its current steady and strong;
Windrows turning here and there to the wind's shifting song.
All I want is a north wind day, everything crisp and clear;
A loon's call, a heron's complaint, and I there to hear.
I'll not get up to the River again, my gypsy life is done.
I'm not certain whom to blame – cancer and old age have won.
All I asked were northern lights or a full moon rising
Before I hit that final shoal, knew the last capsizing.

Passing the Horizon

Moonrise or northern light
And one loon calling me,
And may there be no tears or further fight
When I head toward the sea.

Just let the flowing River take me home.
No sirens and no horn.
No dredging depths or searchlights through the foam.
No call to mourn.

Star shine or channel bell,
And then the lightless dark,
The soundless depths beyond the knell
Of human lark.

I've had my time, my place, my River life,
And when I'm called to leave,
All I ask is a simple drum and fife,
Or one guitar to grieve.

Composed at Harry Gray Cancer Center, October 30, 2009

Life has not anything to show less fair.
Dull would he be of wits who could not see
the terror in our eyes who've come to be
weighed, stuck and bled, all secrets bare.
"Buck up," "Look on the bright side" in the air —
"Your families, parents, children all love thee;
when you get home they'll brew a pot of tea."
Forget how hard they struggle not to stare.
Never did shock and fear more starkly show
than on the faces of these blind-sided souls.
A horror worse than any conjured by Poe.
Not to be calmed by valleys, bridge or knolls.
"Dear God!" is right. The reaper's poised to mow.
All our boats are headed straight for shoals.

How Do I Hate Thee?

How do I hate Thee? I cannot count the ways.
I hate Thee with the muscle and the might
My body traps when falling out of light
And hope and joy and comfort, even space.
I'll hate Thee to the bottom of my days,
Steadfast in claiming Thou did not have the right
To sneak into my blood some brooding night
And twist my path into a sunken maze.
I hate Thee with the energy I kept
For children, peace, and justice all around.
I hate Thee for the way Thou held me prepped —
Seven years, I'm told, 'til Thou were found —
Thou so adept and I so damned inept.
I'll only hate Thee more from underground.

Ridi, Pagliaccia

Laugh, lady, you're still a housewife.
Put on your slippers, your apron and clean.
Never mind what's dirty inside.
This is your life, so laugh, lady.

Hey, lady, you are a healer.
Look each in the eye and try to be wise.
Ignore your doubts and dizzy confusion.
This is your job. Do it, lady.

What, lady? You are a poet?
Pick up your pencil and paper and write.
Even in pain and rising terror,
This is your calling. Create, lady.

Sitting in My Rocker in My Own House in West Hartford, Connecticut

Out my front window I watch light move
over my neighbor's house,
oak leaves down, raked up,
bagged and trucked away.
Leaf blowers whining down on Fern Street
make morning no glory, more a pain.
To my right,
in my untended yard 'neath drooping firs
the dropping cones pile up,
monuments to my undone chores.
I lean back. As the day passes and night comes on,
rodents chitter, gnawing into my home.
I must fight for my life.

The Road Not Chosen

Two trails took off in mid-July.
Sorry, I was not in on the plan.
I would have chosen the one heading high,
but I was not offered that choice, not I,
and the road I got given is one I would ban.

The first would have led me to New Book City,
and readings and signings and sales and praise.
I got to look up it, but, oh, the pity,
the path I was sent on is really shitty
and has me still in a daze in a maze.

For I got shoved onto the cancer trail —
the biopsy, catscanning, bloodletting route
through the finger-prick, CVP, lymphoma vale
where there is no trial and there is no bail,
and the nodes in charge do not give a hoot.

So, Bobby, you sigh as you tell your story,
now that you're ages and ages hence.
I feel as though I have been struck by a lorry,
caught in the headlights, a targetted quarry,
with no chance to choose that difference.

Rage, Idle Rage

Rage, idle rage, I know now how it feels.
Rage from the gut of long-avoided fears
Rises in the eyes and forms upon the tongue.
I'm looking at the days that came before
And thinking of the nights that might yet be.

New as the playmates met before we walked,
My memory brings them back from where they've gone.
And small as the ones I kissed on fields of play
When love was simple: laugh and dance and run—
Before I knew of nights that might yet be.

Ah, sad to think of wasted summer dawns
When loving touch lost to hungover snarls,
Yet healthy bodies thought they'd always be
Ready some other mornings for full joy,
Never imagining nights that might yet be.

Odd to realize cancer's pulled the plug
And let the flood of lost and missed and never
Wipe out what seemed and even, sometimes, was.
The only bird that sings is that mourning dove
Warning of all the nights that might yet be.

Mimicry of the Doc's Ekphrasticism

Somehow the poet
puts Brueghel's season
in question

maybe the farmer
was done
the strenuous ploughing

a sign that winter
advanced creeping
near

the seaside scene
unconcerned
with anyone

scurrying under the sun
what melted
the wing's wax

more significantly
might have been
a cancer

so Icarus died unknowing
dead
before drowning

Museo de Bella Lymphoma

About suffering, they were sometimes right,
The old masters: not that they really knew
The fine details: how it scores points in secret,
Not always advertising, promoting or even disclosing the fight.
How, when someone is eagerly, lovingly living,
With friendships, passionate callings, and places to be,
With grandchildren coming, growing, laughing, always forgiving.
Cancer destroys this world.
They usually forgot
That ordinary lives aren't out to save
Or fancy they are martyrs to be shot
To rescue the world or someone's dog or free a slave,
Themselves innocent as a horse 'neath a tree.

From Auden's poem, for instance, one would never guess
The ploughman is distracted by distress:
Lymphoma cells have invaded his gut.
He keeps on working, hoping to keep on feeding his kin.
So, yes, he failed to notice that falling boy,
And did not call out to that passing ship "Yo! Ahoy!"
For all we know that captain's got cancer of the butt
And is lying bunked with pain-relieving gin.

Lymphoma

Lymphoma, who made you?
Does anyone know who made you?
Gave you power and bade you feed
On those who really do not need
To give you sustenance and cells
While you send them to private hells;
Gave you such an appetite
That some are eaten without a fight.
Lymphoma, who made you?
Does anyone know who made you?

Lymphoma, I will tell you!
Lymphoma, we will tell you!
He is not called by your name,
He is known by his game.
You pretend to be so mild,
Innocent as any child.
I an old woman and you a scam,
Nibbling around like a little lamb.
Lymphoma, the Devil made you.
Lymphoma: Devil take you.

To the Patients, To Make a Lot of Noise

Rip off the lilacs now, and, hey,
Snatch that wisteria, shouting;
It's better to flaunt the blooms today
Than ever to go down pouting.

The earth, the moon, go 'round and 'round,
Our journey's but a loner;
Too soon we'll all be underground,
So why go down a moaner?

Whatever age you've reached is best.
Since cancer's always waiting,
Don't kill time cleaning up the nest:
Get on with dating, mating.

Don't hesitate, don't duck your head,
You have no time for biding.
The life you've led will equal zed
If you continue hiding.

My Lymphoma's Dance

The foulness of my tongue
Should make my partner queasy,
But cancer's ever young,
His dance is never easy.

We sashay through the kitchen,
Step out along the hall.
I'm the one who's bitchin'.
Cancer will not fall.

The grip that holds me tight
Pretends there is no crime
And spins me half the night,
Faking a timing rhyme.

I'm beaten on my head
Just like a battered wife;
Yet, I waltz off to bed
Still hanging on for life.

To Lymphoma, On Our Ongoing War

Tell me not, cancer, that I am wrong
To doubt the innocence
Of your intruding where you don't belong —
And your quiet violence.

Yes, you tricked me into calm —
I am so slow to learn —
You almost got title to embalm
Or burn me into an urn.

And yet, at last, I knew your clutch
And understood the score:
   I could not hate Thee, dear, so much
   Loved I not living more.

Cancer Poetics

Cancer should be reticent and weak
In retreat from peak,

Worn
As old ones ready to be reborn,

Weakened as the rotting limbs
Of tired priests whimpering their final hymns —

Cancer should be hapless
As ancient hardened sap.

Cancer should be stopped in time
Not be a solved crime,

Dying as the days clear up
Cell by cell the life-desiring nodes,

Dying, though the night would try to find,
And beat the nodes to death before the dawn —

Cancer should be stopped in time
Not be a solved crime.

Cancer should be whipped:
Not quipped.

For all the tales of battles pitched
An empty bed and a lover ditched.

For hope
A heron waiting and a loon's clear call —

Cancer should not be.
It's mean.

My Rage Be Still

My Rage, be still! These are the last
Words that you and I shall waste.
Let's end what we had once begun;
For when this poem is out and past,
Rage, be still, for I am done.

Hope to be heard, if just by one,
Before my name is carved in stone.
If these poems touch the core of none
Need we hate ourselves and run?
No, no, Rage, for we are done.

No cliff resists the raging sea
More firmly than we resisted Thee,
Lymphoma, you barbarian hun.
I may yet prove past remedy.
Still, Rage, you and I are done.

Proud about others who fought and lost,
Simple souls whom Cancer bossed,
Lymphoma struts and claims to have won.
Don't think all anger has been tossed
Just because Rage and I are done.

Cancer, you'll be caught someday.
Science will corner you, you'll pay,
Cowering, naked, under the sun,
Too weak to hurt the kids at play
Even though Rage and I are done.

Perhaps you'll hang on, withered and weak,
Your former roar reduced to a squeak,
Whimpering piteously 'neath the moon.
Long may your dying cells leak.
I'll care not. Rage and I are done.

Perhaps you'll get a brief comeback
And hassle a few like some old quack
Proclaiming your secret powers to stun.
Then you'll discover you've lost the knack.
Keep on. Rage and I are done.

So calm down, Rage. This is the last
Verse that you and I shall waste.
I'm ending what we had once begun.
Now are the poems finished and past.
Rage, be still, for I am done.

AFTERWORD

The Watcher

There is silence over the River now.
Time has passed, as it does.
I've done all I was told to do.
Scans and tests look good.
You and I know that you're still here,
but for now, the bay is mine.
Lymphoma, oh, Lymphoma,
I am the watcher now.

INSPIRATIONS

Big Lymphoma (5). *Richard Cory,* Edward Arlington Robinson.

Cancer is A'Coming In (6). *Sumer is icumen in,* anonymous. [W. deWycombe?]

On First Being Diagnosed Stage Three (7). *On First Looking into Chapman's Homer,* John Keats.

Rondel of Merciless Hurt (8). *Rondel of Merciless Beauty,* Geoffrey Chaucer.

Bigger Lymphoma (9). *Ozymandias,* Percy Bysshe Shelley.

Spotted Rashy (10). *Pied Beauty,* Gerard Manley Hopkins.

J.D., You Go and Catch a Star (11). *Go and Catch a Falling Star,* John Donne.

The White, White Dandelion (12). *A Red, Red Rose,* Robert Burns.

No Comment (13). *Comment,* Dorothy Parker.

Snapshot (14). *Buffalo Bill's defunct,* e.e. cummings.

The Tyrant of Lymphoma (15). *The Emperor of Ice Cream,* Wallace Stevens.

Sneak, Sneak, Sneak (16). *Break, Break, Break,* Alfred, Lord Tennyson.

Like Her I Said to Hell with Death (17). *Because I Would Not Stop For Death,* Emily Dickinson.

I Thought I'd Master'd the Trodden Ways (18). *She Dwelt Among The Untrodden Ways,* William Wordsworth.

Cancer, Get Over It (19). *Death, Be Not Proud,* John Donne.

The River Island of Set Me Free (20). *The Lake Isle of Innisfree,* William Butler Yeats.

Cancer Loves Me, This I Know (21). *Jesus Loves Me,* Anna Bartlett Warner and Susan Warner.

The Sneak That From The Old Root Sucks the Flower (22). *The Force That Through The Green Fuse Drives The Flower,* Dylan Thomas.

This Is Not To Say (23). *This Is Just To Say,* William Carlos Williams.

This Time of Life (24). *That Time of Year Thou Mayst in Me Behold,* Sonnet 73, William Shakespeare.

Under Night's Cover (25). Whenas In Silks My Julia Goes, Robert Herrick.

River Sickness (26). *Sea Fever,* John Masefield.

Passing the Horizon (27). *Crossing the Bar,* Alfred, Lord Tennyson.

Composed At Harry Gray Cancer Center, October 30, 2009 (28). *Composed Upon Westminster Bridge, September 3, 1802,* William Wordsworth.

How Do I Hate Thee? (29). *How Do I Love Thee?* Elizabeth Barrett Browning.

Ridi, Pagliaccia (30). *Vesti la Giubba,* Ruggiero Leoncavallo.

Sitting in my Rocker in My Own House in West Hartford, Connecticut (31). *Lying in My Hammock at William Duffy's Farm in Pine Island,* James Wright.

The Road Not Chosen (32). *The Road Not Taken,* Robert Frost.

Rage, Idle Rage (33). *Tears, Idle Tears,* Alfred, Lord Tennyson.

Mimicry of the Doc's Ekphrasticism (34). *Landscape with the Fall of Icarus,* William Carlos Williams.

Museo de Bella Lymphoma (35). *Musée des Beaux Arts,* W. H. Auden.

Lymphoma (36). *The Lamb,* William Blake.

To the Patients, To Make a Lot of Noise (37). *To the Virgins, To Make Much of Time,* Robert Herrick.

My Lymphoma's Dance (38). *My Papa's Waltz,* Theodore Roethke.

To Lymphoma, On Our Ongoing War (39). *To Lucasta, Going To The Wars,* Richard Lovelace.

Cancer Poetics (40). *Ars Poetica,* Archibald MacLeish.

My Rage Be Still (42). *My Lute Awake,* Sir Thomas Wyatt.

ABOUT THE AUTHOR

Elizabeth Kincaid-Ehlers moved to Connecticut in 1979 to be Visiting Writer-in-Residence at Trinity College for one year. She came to like living in Connecticut so much during an extension of her contract that when it ended, she went back to school and retrained as a psychotherapist in order to stay in the state. During her years of additional studies, she taught at the Hartford branch of the University of Connecticut and participated in the state's Writers-in-the-Schools Program.

Elizabeth was born in Michigan and, after spending part of her growing-up years in Georgia, she went back north to earn her B.A. at the University of Michigan in 1955. Throughout the following years, because of her husband's peregrinations, Elizabeth began many M.A. programs, only to have to abandon credits and move on. At last the family, which by then included two sons, stayed still long enough for her to earn an M.A. at the University of Illinois. After a move to Rochester, New York, and the birth of two more sons, the marriage ended. Elizabeth then went on to earn a Ph.D. at the University of Rochester in 1978. During all those years she continued to teach and write.

Since the mid-1980s, Elizabeth has maintained a private practice as a psychotherapist, all the while writing, giving poetry readings, and occasionally teaching. Her oldest son and family remain in upstate New York, while the three other sons and their wives live in the Hartford area, along with her five, and counting, younger grand-children. For them she is constantly grateful. Furthermore, for love of them, she intends to stay put.

ABOUT THE BOOK

This book is set in Garamond Premier Pro, which had its genesis in 1988 when type-designer Robert Slimbach visited the Plantin-Moretus Museum in Antwerp, Belgium, to study its collection of Claude Garamond's metal punches and typefaces. During the mid-fifteen hundreds, Garamond—a Parisian punch-cutter—produced a refined array of book types that combined an unprecedented degree of balance and elegance, for centuries standing as the pinnacle of beauty and practicality in type-founding. Slimbach has created an entirely new interpretation based on Garamond's designs and on comparable italics cut by Robert Granjon, Garamond's contemporary.

To order additional copies of this book
or other Antrim House titles, contact the publisher at

Antrim House
21 Goodrich Rd., Simsbury, CT 06070
860.217.0023, AntrimHouse@comcast.net
or the house website (www.AntrimHouseBooks.com).

•

On the house website
are sample poems, upcoming events,
and a "seminar room" featuring supplemental biography,
notes, images, poems, reviews, and
writing suggestions.